YOUR KNOWLEDGE HAS

- We will publish your bachelor's and
  master's thesis, essays and papers

- Your own eBook and book -
  sold worldwide in all relevant shops

- Earn money with each sale

Upload your text at www.GRIN.com
and publish for free

Shady Selim

Usability - The key for success or failure of web projects

GRIN Verlag

Bibliografische Information der Deutschen Nationalbibliothek:

Die Deutsche Bibliothek verzeichnet diese Publikation in der Deutschen National-
bibliografie; detaillierte bibliografische Daten sind im Internet über http://dnb.d-
nb.de/ abrufbar.

Imprint:

Copyright © 2010 GRIN Verlag GmbH
Druck und Bindung: Books on Demand GmbH, Norderstedt Germany
ISBN: 978-3-656-22554-6

This book at GRIN:

http://www.grin.com/en/e-book/196416/usability-the-key-for-success-or-failure-of-
web-projects

Usability: the key for success or failure of web projects

Shady Yehia Yassin Mohamed Selim

1/9/2010

"A thesis submitted in partial fulfilment of the requirements for the degree of Master of Science in Business Information Technology."

ABSTRACT

Many websites are published daily and others are removed. A normal web surfer can notice many websites that deliver similar services, but only one or two of them are distinguished and have higher visits rates, while others are poorly noticed or remembered.

Different studies have been made to determine the keys of success or failure of web projects. This study aims to investigate web sites usability, and draw attention to usability as key factor in positioning websites in ranking charts, encouraging visitors' web traffic, and keeping visitors' loyalty. Commercial web sites, services web sites and portals aim to increase their benefits and income, so this study will introduce usability as a most important factor for achieving this, and making web sites and projects stand out from others.

For those who are not familiar with the term web usability, this study will first introduce the web usability definition, and then web sites usability history will be briefly discussed. The study will also point out the importance of web usability testing methodology, and describe some of these methodologies.

The '*Drupal*' content management system is employed in. A practical case study to apply usability to determine the effort made in usability testing, and the reflection of usability testing on it. This study points out how usability testing efforts was a key of success in helping this product to top its competitors.

An online survey was conducted to collect web surfers' data about their understanding of usability, and their attitude towards it. The results have been analysed and charts were drawn, to visualise the collected data information.

Conclusions had drawn summarizing the study, and the survey analysis results, discovering that usability helps to increase the revenue of web sites owners. Future work is mentioned too, containing the points that could add more value to this study, and contributions that could be added or other researches can take as starting points to make complementary work.

1

INTRODUCTION

When Microsoft Office 2007 and Windows Vista were first introduced, even though they seemed great for new users with the latest User Interface technologies, they raised a lot of questions and frustrations for old ones, because they did not abide the simplest rules of usability like anticipation, for example by changing the simple familiar menus in Microsoft Office 2007 and replacing it with the ribbon (Joel, 2007; Paul, 2008; Excel Spreadsheet Authors, 2010).

Usability is "the study of the ease with which people can employ a particular tool or other human-made object in order to achieve a particular goal" (Wikipedia, 2010). This is the simplest description.

Web usability, which is the subject of this study, is more specific to web sites design usefulness and easiness, to enhance the simplicity and clarity of them for web surfers or visitors. Visitors likes to interact with web sites immediately, and do not appreciate searching for help pages on how to use these web sites (Wikipedia, 2010).

Figure a: (Shari and Nick, 2009 p.21)

The previous figure is from Shari and Nick. It was to describe the Google searcher unwanted reaction if the chosen web site does not have the required information (Shari and Nick, 2009 p.21). But it was suitable also to demonstrate the surfer feeling who can not interact or understand a web site because the lack of its usability, so I wanted to use it in that context, in an attempt to picture the idea.

Peter Seebach wrote an important article, declaring the importance of usability in software development and designing. He pointed out that more effort and money were spent on games design usability, in comparison to productivity software design. He encouraged learning usability lessons from arcade designers. He also pointed out the deficiencies in productivity software streamlining, reliability, and approachability, in comparison to arcade games (Peter Seebach, 2002).

In researches, studies, and journals usability could also be referred to as 'user experience' or 'UX'. Also other researches referred to usability and user experience as two separate things with intertwined relationships (Effie L.-C. Law and Paul van Schaik 2010), and others related usability to 'Human-Computer Interaction' or 'HCI' (Jacko, 2007).

WEB USABILITY

Benefits

As Steve Krug noted, 'People won't use Web Sites if they can't find their way around it' (2005, p.51). The first benefit is saving web visitors loyalty. By making the web site user and reader friendly with clear navigation and well structured content, this will encourage web visitors revisits (Terry Sullivan, 1997).

The second benefit is increasing web sites revenue and improving the return of investment 'ROI'. Web usability achieves this by easing the way web visitors of commercial web site find the items they want to buy, by offering recommended products, and by increasing the percentage the web site visitors whom would complete their purchase (Jakob Nielsen 2000). ROI could also be achieved by reducing customer service calls, or by saving production time by reducing error rate and the time needed to complete a task (Usability First, 2010; Ying Zou et al, 2007).

Other benefit is enhancing the web site ranking on search engines. This can be achieved by advertising the web site information in the right way, and optimising web site data for search engines, by making the site search engine friendly, to help to get the right user, by anticipating search engines behaviours and search engines users' behaviours (Shari and Nick, 2009).

Evaluation and Testing

Many researches contributed by introducing methods for usability testing. John Brooke, for example, came up with the System Usability Scale or 'SUS' as a part of a usability engineering programme, because as he stated the need for "quick and dirty" ways to permit low cost usability assessments in industrial systems evaluation (Brooke,1996).

Conceptual frameworks were also introduced by J.I. Van Kuijk and his colleagues for case study research in usability. They visualised the framework, which was a slightly detailed, and a bit complex looking structure, nevertheless, the visualised framework proved a very valuable tool during the data processing and the setup of the case study research. The core of the framework is the product development process, as a part of the human-product interaction. They recognized six actors which activities and methods should be investigated because of their likely effect on usability in product development process (J.I. Van Kuijk et al, 2007).

Jakob Nielsen

He is one of the leaders of web usability, and the most famous among them. He contributed with a lot of books, publications, and articles. Even though some designers contradicted his methods like Zhang P. and Von Dran (2000), but almost all usability researchers refer to his books and studies.

In his conference paper 'Usability Inspection Methods', Jacob summarized the most famous usability testing methods, as quoted from his paper:

- Heuristic evaluation is the most informal method and involves having usability specialists judge whether each dialogue element follows established usability principles (the "heuristics").
- Heuristic estimation is a variant in which the inspectors are asked to estimate the relative usability of two (or more) designs in quantitative terms (typically expected user performance).
- Cognitive walkthrough uses a more explicitly detailed procedure to simulate a user's problem-solving process at each step through the dialogue, checking if the simulated user's goals and memory content can be assumed to lead to the next correct action.
- Pluralistic walkthrough uses group meetings where users, developers, and human factors people step through a scenario, discussing each dialogue element.
- Feature inspection lists sequences of features used to accomplish typical tasks, checks for long sequences, cumbersome steps, steps that would not be natural for users to try,

3

and steps that require extensive knowledge/experience in order to assess a proposed feature set.

- Consistency inspection has designers who represent multiple other projects inspect an interface to see whether it does things in the same way as their own designs.
- Standards inspection has an expert on an interface standard inspect the interface for compliance.
- Formal usability inspection combines individual and group inspections in a six-step procedure with strictly defined roles to with elements of both heuristic evaluation and a simplified form of cognitive walkthroughs.

(Jakob Nielsen, 1994)

Jakob stated that none of these methods is the best or surpass those others, but the project and the budget are what decide the best method to use. He also stated that the best results can often be achieved by combining more than one of these methods, and that using usability specialists helps in getting better results (1994).

UNDERSTAND YOUR USER

To achieve a successful web site some considerations and actions should be taken in advance. The first is to determine the web sites targeted user or audience, and then study their behaviour and needs.

What the User Wants

Lund stated some considerations in evaluating the design and usability of a website,

- Know the user, and YOU are not the user.
- Things that look the same should act the same.
- The information for the decision needs to be there when the decision is needed.
- Error messages should actually mean something to the user and tell the user how to fix the problem.
- Every action should have a reaction.
- Everyone makes mistakes, so every mistake should be fixable.
- Don't overload the user's buffers.
- Consistency, consistency, consistency.
- Minimize the need for a mighty memory.
- Keep it simple.
- The user should always know what is happening.
- The more you do something, the easier it should be to do.
- The user should control the system. The system should not control the user. The user is the boss and the system should show it.
- Eliminate unnecessary decisions and illuminate the rest.
- The best journey is the one with fewest steps. Shorten the distance between the user and the goal.
- The user should be able to do what the user wants to do.
- If I made an error, let me know about it before I get into REAL trouble.
- You should always know how to find out what to do next.
- The idea is to empower the user, not speed up the system.
- Things that look different should act different.

(Wikipedia, 2010)

Usability Differs by Gender

If creating a web site to target female users, some changes have to be done, and some considerations have to be taken.

Using a comScore whitepaper (Linda Boland Abraham et al, 2010), Frank Spillers made a useful study about the gender differences in web usability (2010).

Frank came out with these key finding from the whitepaper:

1. Women have surpassed men as online buyers (and they spend more) and their influencing is growing rapidly, in addition to the use of group buying or 'flash sale' sites (e.g. Groupon.com LivingSocial.com). Social retail is an emerging area for women, due to their tendency to share and discuss with other others.

2. Women spend more time online (8% globally) than men and 30% more time on social networking sites than men.

3. Women are motivated differently in their use of social networking sites like Twitter. Twitter adoption is equal or higher than men. Twitter is used by women more for conversation, to follow celebrities or to find deals and promotions. Men are more likely to post their own tweets.

4. Social networking is emerging as a driver for women in the mobile sphere.

5. Women are using online entertainment (e.g. puzzle, board and card games) and functional sites (money management) as much as men (change in past behavior where health, apparel, baby goods).

6. Cultural differences in emerging markets (Asia, Latin America) will always influence online behavior by gender- an important localization issue.

7. Older women moreover men, are rapidly adopting social networking sites-- and at the same intensity of younger women.

8. Women are still attracted to health content, community and lifestyle sites. However women are outpacing men in some areas of finance and are actively engaging in male-dominated areas: adult content and gambling.

9. Compared to men, women Bing users spend more time on Bing for search, than Google- and YouTube for video. Facebook, while visited more than men is unable to compete with regional social networking sites (such as CyWorld in South Korea, Vkontakte.ru in Russia, Mixi.jp in Japan or StudiVZ in Germany), especially among older women.

10. Women spend more time on Social Networking, Instant Messaging (IM) and Email than men globally.

11. The embrace of social networking and its importance to women has significant implications for content and user experience.

12. Women spend more time on photo sites and adopt photo sharing faster. Email usage is higher in the 45+ age group. Latin American women do more IM'ing than other women globally, with their use of email topping North American females.
(Frank Spillers, 2010)

Frank also declared that men like fast sites while women prefer the ones with easy of use and navigation, and pointed to his personal experience in women demand to add extra pink tab for women's content in a male web site (2010).

The User's Eye Behaviour
This is called eye tracking. New equipments are now available to monitor the user's eye, record its movement, and what areas attracts the user's eye, and what areas it ignores (Christi O'Connell, 2010).

Studying eye tracking can help web designers to decide how to arrange web pages contents, and what users see and ignore in their designs.

Different eye movements' patterns were discovered. Nielson stated that eye moves across the page in F-Shape pattern (Christi O'Connell, 2010). Nielson also advised to put the most important information in the first two paragraphs, because web sites visitors scans web pages quickly and do not read all the contents (Christi O'Connell, 2010).

Shrestha came out with the eye gaze pattern, stating that eye gaze in browsing or searching text-based pages differs from picture-based pages. He also noticed that users who browse picture-based pages begin from right to left down until they reached the bottom of the page, while those who search the same pages their eyes were less systematic jumping all over the page till find what they are searching for, and while searching, the F-Shaped pattern was not there (Christi O'Connell, 2010).

Shrestha also made comparison between one-column and two-column web pages, discovering that two-column web pages are more likely to be read (Christi O'Connell, 2010).

Nielsen discovered that users rarely take their eyes off the content, and hardly ever look at banner advertisements, and that users scan fancy formatted text without actually reading it (Christi O'Connell, 2010).

The User is a Scanner Not a Surfer

Web users scan pages rather that reading it. In his book, Steve noted that while web designer might consider a web page has great information or data, users interact with it like "billboard going by at 60 miles an hour" (Steve Krug, 2005, p.21).

Steve mentioned that users do not make best choices but rather reasonable ones, and that they do not really have any idea how things work but they muddle through (2005, p.20-45).

He advised designers to make sure to distinctive data with clear hierarchy, to replace words with conventions, visually break the web page apart, differentiate clickable parts, keep the background clear, minimize web pages instructions, and the most to get rid of half the words on each page, then get rid of half of what's left (Steve Krug, 2005, p.20-45).

Conclusion

The previous sections proved the importance for web sites owners to study the behaviours of their web sites targeted audience, and how the design should be different according to the targeted audience gender. Web sites designers should understand what the user wants, and learn how users scan web pages content.

These are a must study and take care notes for web designers and web sites owners to make sure that users receive the intended messages, keep their loyalty, make them notice web sites paid advertisement and new announcements, and results to increase their web sites return of investments.

DRUPAL AND USABILITY

Drupal is an open source content management system 'CMS' made by Dr. Dries Buytaert in year 2000, and released as open source by January 2001 (Drupal, 2010).

The reason of choosing Drupal as a case study is, even though this web solution is as new as from 2001, in comparison to other older content management system solutions, but it managed to surpass the other competitors in few years, and gaining awards as being the best content management system (Packt Publishing, 2010).

To achieve this, and because Dries stressed that developers and designers should "Continue to make Drupal easier to use" (Jimmy Berry, 2008; Dries Buytaert, 2008), developers made intensive usability testing and provided "a suite of usability testing tools that will allow data to be recorded and analyzed in order to make improvements to Drupal's usability" (Jimmy Berry, 2008), and designers used the University of Baltimore and the University of Minnesota Office for Information Technology's usability lab to conduct formal usability testing on Drupal, by the means of recording eye-tracking data and video (Dries Buytaert, 2008; Thomas Moseler, 2008).

In his conference booklet, Thomas described how they conducted user usability tests at the University of Minnesota, with whom, and how, in 72 interesting slide. The great about these slides that is shows a real life case scenario of implementing usability tests with results, remarks, and learned lessons that were corrected. Thomas mentioned the tools they used, how they created the testing environment, and what sort of data they collected, and how they collected it, and the lessons they learned from it (2008).

Because Drupal team from developers and designers learned the lesson about the importance of usability, Drupal is know the first choice for a lot of personal, commercial, and even governmental web sites and portals (Eche, 2007).

As mentioned above, even though Drupal testing were made by other parties, but the reason of bringing it in this study is to bring a real life success case of using usability to enhance a web site or web project. This was proven in this section how usability helped Drupal to learn about its mistakes by the performing tests, correcting its usability mistakes, and how this affected it positively to reach its current advance position among other competitors, wining awards, and become the first choice for small and big web applications owners.

THE SURVEY

To collect recent updated real life data to analyze for my study, this survey was formulated and conducted online, and invitation e-mails were sent to various personals describing the purpose of this survey.

Twenty participants completed successfully the survey out of 32 visitors. All of the participants were from the Middle East region - the importance of stating this information will be drawn later.

The questions were selected after reviewing several books and articles on usability and others on survey designing. The aim of this survey was to check the participants' previous knowledge of usability, their awareness of it when checking a new web site, how usability affects their decisions in selecting particular web sites or services, if they think that this survey questions contributed to their knowledge, and if it helped in changing the way they will look to their current and future visited web sites. Of course the first four questions were to check that the survey participates are good divert samples to represent the web users.

Charts were also drawn to visualise the survey collected data, with explanation of the results.

Survey Results

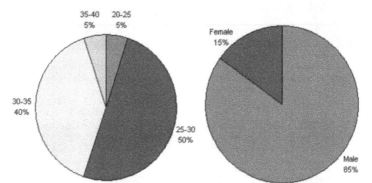

Figure 1: Participants' ages ranges in years   *Figure 2*: Participants' genders

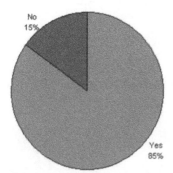

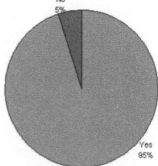

Figure 3: If participants' jobs are related to the internet

Figure 4: Participants' previous knowledge of usability

9

As mentioned, the first four charts give information about the participants themselves, to determine if the collected sample is good enough in variety. From figure 1 it shows that participants' ages are not too old or too young, so their ages are suitable to analyze and make decisions. Figure 2 two shows that participant females are less than males, but are acceptable. In figure 3 it shows that not all the participants work in related job to the internet industry, and that is good because casual not professional web surfers participated too in this survey. Participants' knowledge in figure 4 is high, but knowledge is not evidence of practice.

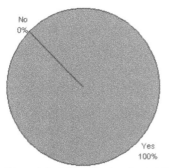

Figure 5: Participants' caring about visited sites usability

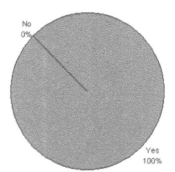

Figure 6: If web sites usability affects on the time participants spend on it

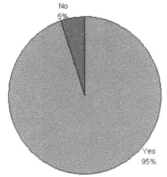

Figure 7: If the site usability affects participants' decision of revisiting it

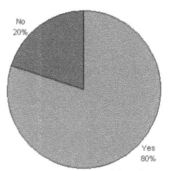

Figure 8: In case the participant has to visit a site in frequent bases, if usability will affect their number of revisits

Figure 5 and figure 6 shows that all participants care about web sites usability, and that it affects the time they spent on web sites. Even though figure 7 shows that most participants decisions of visiting web sites are affected my usability, in figure 8 less participants stated that their visits will be affected by usability if the web sites is related to work.

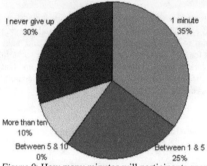

Figure 9: How many minutes will participants spend on a site searching for a link before giving up and closing the page

In figure 9, 35% of the participants declared that they would only search for one minute for the requested link on a web site before giving up and either close it or switch to other web site, and 25% will give up in five minutes, while 10% will wait for ten minutes before giving up. The rest 30% of the participants stated that they will never give up till they find the information they need.

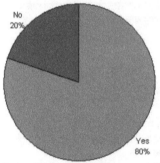

Figure 10: In selecting a news portal, if design affects the participants' decision

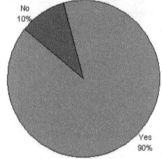

Figure 11: In selecting a news portal, if news source affects on participants' decision

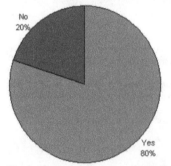

Figure 12: In selecting a news portal, if site's usability affects on participants' decision

Figures 10, 11, and 12 are answering questions about what affects on the participants in selecting news portals as source of news. Figure 10 and figure 12 shows that most participants' choices are affected by the portal design and usability. In figure 11 more participants' decision were affected by the news portal news source.

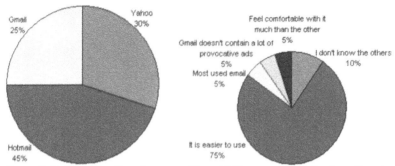

Figure 13: Participants' mail service   *Figure 14*: The reason of selecting the mail service

Figure 13 and figure 14 to learn what makes the participants select their mail service. In figure 14, 75% of the participants stated that mail service interface easiness is the reason, while 10% declared that the reason is that they do not know the other services and subscribed with what they know. The rest reasons with equal 5% portion were because, their service does not force ads, their service is more famous, and because they feel comfortable with it.

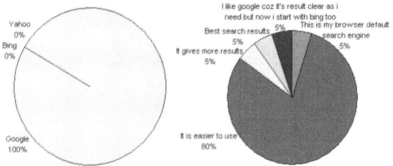

Figure 15: Participants' search engine   *Figure 16*: The reason of selecting the search engine

In selecting the search engine, in figure 15 and figure 16, 80% selected their search engine for its easiness, and the rest with equal 5% portion reasons were because of their preferred search engine number of results, their feelings that it is the best search engine, because their search engine gives clearer results, and because it is their browsers default search engine.

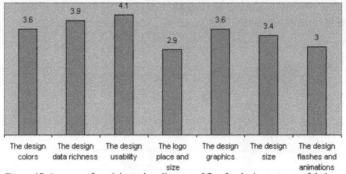

Figure 17: Average of participants' scaling out of five for the importance of their own sites contents (The highest the most important)

Figure 17 is answering the question if the participants own web sites and need to select design for them; about the main factors that will affect on their decision from scale one to five as five is the highest. According to the participates, the highest to the lowest importance in order were: The design usability, the design data richness, the design colours, the design graphics, the design size, the design flashes and animations, the logo place and size.

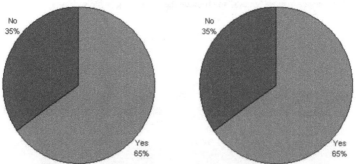

Figure 18: Participants' knowledge of Web 2.0   *Figure 19*: If participants knew that Web 2.0 enhance usability

Figure 18 and figure 19, shows that only 65% knew what Web 2.0 term means, notices it in web sites designs, and knew that it enhances web sites usability.

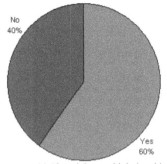 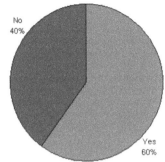

Figure 20: If participants think that this survey helped them learning more about usability and Web 2.0

Figure 21: If participants think that this survey changed the way that they will look to websites

In figure 20 and figure 21, 60% of the participants declared that this survey helped them learning more about usability and Web 2.0, and that this survey changed the way that they will look to websites.

Survey Analysis

By agreeing that this sample represents web surfers, the survey shows that most of the web surfers do care about web usability, and that their decisions to revisit web sites are affected by its usability, even if these web sites related to work.

The survey also shows that most the web visitors if they could not find the information they need quickly or had difficulty finding the links they want, they will leave the web site for another.

Even though most web visitors care about web sites design and usability and it affects on their decision in selecting their data source sites, they care more about web sites data. So they find design and usability important but data is more important.

What affects most web visitors to select a web service or prefer a service provider on another like search engine and web mail providers is its easiness of use or usability.

Not all web visitors even though who work in the internet and web fields knows new web technologies like Web 2.0 and do not know that it increase web sites usability, which shows that only few monitors the new in the usability trends and technologies, even those who work in the web field.

More than half the participant found that this survey useful, enlightened them, add to their knowledge, changed the way they will look to web sites before and after the survey.

Thus the importance of spreading usability awareness and teaching its techniques are proven. This should lead to make web sites designers keen to learn web usability to satisfy their audience, web development companies to hire web usability specialists, web usability services companies to open, and web sites owners to be careful and aware for their sites usability as they are for its contents, colours, images, and search engine optimisations.

CONCLUSION

Current studies, articles, and books on usability tackle its methodologies and testing techniques, but almost none pointed usability as an important key for success or failure for web sites or application, and the aim of this study is to draw attention and prove this point of study.

After defining the meaning of web usability, its benefits, and different methods of testing it, then pointing out how web user interact with web sites, a real life product was employed in to prove the usefulness of usability testing in improving web projects position among competitors. Also a survey was conducted to collect real web users' direct opinion about the usefulness and importance of web usability according to their opinions.

As shown in this study that usability can help in increasing the percentage of a commercial web site visitors who complete a purchase (Jakob Nielsen, 2000), in reducing time spent to accomplish task in e-commerce application (Ying Zou et al, 2007), in improving the return on investment of web sites (Usability First, 2010), and enhancing web sites presence and ranking on search engines (Shari and Nick, 2009).

'Drupal' the content management system developers and designers greatly benefited from applying usability testing to compete present good competitors, advance it in charts (Thomas Moseler, 2008), wining awards, and attract new customers.

The conducted survey also showed that most web visitors leave web sites with no clear navigations, and prefer web services and solutions that have simpler interaction interface; they do care about usability, and like learn more about it.

Current users do not have time to think or read. They are only scanning web pages, and if they could not find the information they need or the web links to it easily, they will lose interest in these web sites and search for others. That is why they select the web services with easier interface.

So usability helps keeping visitors' loyalty (Terry Sullivan, 1997), and increases the revenue of web sites owners, and advancing web site rank in search engine. This is the real success in the web sites field, and this is the target every web site, web application, or web services owner aims to achieve, and this is the most important point that this study positively proved.

For me, conducting this study contributed so much to my knowledge. Before starting this study I used few simple collected knowledge from web design specialised web articles for judging web designs usability in my work, but while selecting my study topic I discovered that professional technical tests and methods were introduced to test web sites usability, and in the studying process to write this study every new book and article added new knowledge to me, such as how users scan web pages, the F-Shape pattern, that usability differs by gender, and that usability can be used as a method of enhance a web site search engines ranking. Before starting the study I wanted to prove that a key reason of success of some web sites is usability, and know I am certain that this is a fact and more attention should be drawn to it, and the conducted survey helped much to prove this.

FURTHER STUDY

As mentioned before that the survey in this work was conducted in the Middle East region. I believe that this work can get more global credibility if a fellow researcher conducted a similar survey in Asia, Europe, and North America regions.

This work can even be extended to include usability for mobile web applications, which is a new field that needs serious attention for its promising future. Recent interviews were posted, but no academic studies or work had been published yet.

An interesting interview was made with Jeffrey Powers and Vikas Reddy, the founders of *Occipital* and creators of mobile applications, describing how they made a second version of their latest application *RedLaser* a big success, and draw attention of customers and press, after they paid more attention to user experience. In this Interview the reader will find with Jeffrey Powers and Vikas Reddy describing the mistakes developers should not do towards user experience when they try to develop applications or web sites for mobiles, they also stated some learned lessons and advices that should be taken to achieve better user experience (Jeffrey Powers et al 2010).

Another recent interview with Chris Brown 'CEO of *Frudoo*' and Rob Walker 'Managing Director of *Xcite Digital*' describing how usability testing for *Frudoo's* website increased the profit of their mobile line of business (UsabilityNews.com 2010).

Technology ground is still raw but advancing very quickly, and life momentum is getting accelerated, so if we do not try to find methods to deliver these technologies with much easiness, these technologies will not be widely adapted. That is why I wish that fellow researches take usability to new technology grounds, and I intend to do so too.

ACKNOWLEDGMENTS

I hereby wish to thank Dr. Chris Sadler my Module Leader for Postgraduate Computing Project for Information Systems Project in the School of Engineering and Information Science at Middlesex University for his valuable contributions and guidance in making this study more academic. I also thank my wife for supporting me days and nights, and staying up with me till I finished this study.

REFRENCES

Brooke, J. (1996), 'SUS: a "quick and dirty" usability scale' in P. W. Jordan, B. Thomas, B. A. Weerdmeester, & A. L. McClelland *Usability Evaluation in Industry* London: Taylor and Francis.

Christi O'Connell (March 2008) *Eyetracking and Web site Design*. Available from <http://www.usability.gov/articles/newsletter/pubs/032010news.html> (Accessed 1 September 2010)

Dries Buytaert (10 March 2008) *First results from usability testing*. Available from <http://buytaert.net/first-results-from-usability-testing> (Accessed 1 September 2010)

Drupal (10 January 2010) *History*. Available from <http://drupal.org/about/history> (Accessed 1 September 2010)

Eche (10 August 2007) *Content Management System (CMS) Report on Alternatives to Back-End*. Available from <http://openconcept.ca/blog/eche/content_management_system_cms_report_on_alternatives_to_back_end> (Accessed 1 September 2010)

Effie L.-C. Law & Paul van Schaik (2010) 'Modelling user experience - An agenda for research and practice' in *Interacting with Computers* Vol. 22 no.5 pp. 313-322

Excel Spreadsheet Authors (26 Mars 2010) *Excel 2007 Compatibility – Avoid Hair Pulling Frustration When Opening or Saving 2003-2007 Files*. Available from <http://www.excel-spreadsheet-authors.com/excel-2007-compatibility-avoid-hair-pulling-frustrastion-when-opening-or-saving-2003-2007-files.html/> (Accessed 1 September 2010)

Frank Spillers (31 July 2010) *New Study- Gender differences in Web Usability*. Available from <http://www.demystifyingusability.com/2010/07/gender-differences-in-web-usability.html> (Accessed 1 September 2010)

J. I. Van Kuijk et al (2007) *Usability in Product Development: A Conceptual Framework*, the Contemporary Ergonomics 2007, Conference Proceedings of The Ergonomics Society Annual Conference, Nottingham, UK, 17-19 April 2007

Jacko, Julie A. (eds) (2007) *Human-Computer Interaction. Interaction Design and Usability*, 12th International Conference, HCI International 2007, held Beijing, China, 22-27 July 2007, Berlin: Springer

Jakob Nielsen (14 January 2000) *Usability On The Web Isn't A Luxury*. Available from <http://www.informationweek.com/773/web.htm> (Accessed 1 September 2010)

Jakob Nielsen (1994) *Usability Inspection Methods*, Conference companion on Human factors in computing systems, p.413-414, 24-28 April 1994, Boston, Massachusetts, United States

Jeffrey Powers, Vikas Reddy, and Jermy Olson (10 May 2010) *How UX can drive sales in mobile apps*. Available from <http://uxmag.com/strategy/how-ux-can-drive-sales-in-mobile-apps> (Accessed 1 September 2010)

Jimmy Berry (25 April 2008) *Usability Testing Suite*. Available from <http://groups.drupal.org/node/11011> (Accessed 1 September 2010)

Joel Spolsky (20 August 2007) *Even the Office 2007 box has a learning curve*. Available from <http://www.joelonsoftware.com/items/2007/08/18.html> (Accessed 1 September 2010)

Linda Boland Abraham et al (30 June 2010) *Women on the Web: How Women are Shaping the Internet*. Available from <http://www.comscore.com/Press_Events/Presentations_Whitepapers/2010/Women_on_the_Web_How_Women_are_Shaping_the_Internet> (Accessed 1 September 2010)

Packt Publishing (2010) *Open Source CMS Award Previous Winners*. Available from <http://www.packtpub.com/article/open-source-cms-award-previous-winners> (Accessed 1 September 2010)

Paul Woods (2008) *The 10 Most Common User Frustrations in Office 2007... And How You Can Avoid Them*. Available from <http://www.slideshare.net/pwoods/the-10-most-common-user-frustrations-in-office-2007-and-how-you-can-avoid-them-presentation> (Accessed 1 September 2010)

Peter Seebach (1 June 2002) *The cranky user: Everything I need to know about usability, I learned at the arcade*. Available from <http://www.ibm.com/developerworks/web/library/us-cranky17.html> (Accessed 1 September 2010)

Shari Thurow & Nick Musica (2009) *When Search Meets Web Usability* California: New Riders Press

Steve Krug (2005) *Don't Make Me Think: A Common Sense Approach to Web Usability, 2nd Edition* California: New Riders Press

Terry Sullivan (6 September 1997) *The Value of Usability*. Available from <http://www.pantos.org/atw/35679.html> (Accessed 1 September 2010)

Thomas Moseler (23 July 2008) *User Testing in Drupal*. Available from <http://szeged2008.drupalcon.org/program/sessions/user-testing-drupal> (Accessed 1 September 2010)

Usability First (2010) *Usability ROI*. Available from <http://www.usabilityfirst.com/about-usability/usability-roi/> (Accessed 1 September 2010)

UsabilityNews.com (14 August 2010) *Usability testing may improve hit rate of Mobile Advertising*. Available from <http://www.usabilitynews.com/news/article6750.asp> (Accessed 1 September 2010)

Wikipedia (26 August 2010) *Usability*. Available from <http://en.wikipedia.org/wiki/Usability> (Accessed 1 September 2010)

Ying Zou et al (2007) 'Improving the Usability of E-Commerce Applications using Business Processes' in *IEEE Transactions on Software Engineering* Vol. 33 no.12 pp. 837-855

Zhang, P., and Von Dran, G.M. "Satisfiers and dissatisfiers: a two-factor model for Website design and evaluation.", *Journal of the American Society for Information Science* (51:14), December 2000, pp 1253-1268.